Introduction

My name is Brandi Sholar. I have had struggles in my life, but now I am a successful entrepreneur. I'm a franchise owner of a tax company. I own a retail clothing store for women and children. I also have a home health care business. I'm a real estate investor. I'm a mentor and a life coach. Why so many businesses, you ask?

See, I been through so much in my life that even though I'm older, now I was mentally verbally and physically abused. The abuse I have encountered caused my life to be unstable and without structure. Anything I tried to accomplish would get taken right away from my kids and I. This abuse has traumatized me, so becoming an owner of multiple businesses keeps me busy from thinking about the things I been through in life.

I now use my life experiences to help others, anyway I can. One way I do this is to coach other women that are going through what I experienced. Now, I'm writing this book to help you become your own boss. I hope it inspires you to start your journey toward becoming an entrepreneur.

I just want the world to know there is always a brighter side to each day. One of the big lessons I've learned in my life is you have to love yourself and take care of yourself. The other lesson I've learned is to love God with all your heart. Always put God first in anything you do! God has brought me through some horrible times, and now I'm living the best chapters of my life. See, those are just two examples of what I'm going to share with you in this book. I'm going to share many more lessons I've learned on my journey to becoming an entrepreneur. I want to inspire you to do what makes you happy. I know you can be a successful entrepreneur, living a stable, happy life. So, let's get started.

Chapter 1

Let's start by talking about what an entrepreneur is. Do you know? An entrepreneur is a person who starts a new business and usually risks his own money to start this venture. There are many people who are very wealthy entrepreneurs today because they didn't give up. Can you think of someone?
Let's read about four successful entrepreneurs that you will recognize their names and their businesses.
Arianna Huffington struggled to get people to read her work for many years before creating *The Huffington Post*. Imagine the doubt that would fill your mind if your book was rejected by thirty-six publishers the way Arianna's was. She didn't let the doubt stop her. She didn't stop striving toward her dream. The confidence and strength of the mind that she showed allowed her to share *The Huffington Post* with the world.
Jeff Bezos, CEO of Amazon, didn't have an easy path to success. He had to struggle with doubt numerous times as he watched his business ideas fail. His most notable failure was zShops, an online auction site. Still, he didn't let these failures and the doubt they created stop him. Thanks to his confidence and persistence, we now can

shop on Amazon, which has become a household name offering customers a wide variety of items. Jeff Bezos' persistence and his long-awaited success should motivate us to keep trying.

Walt Disney was told a mouse would never work. Before Walt Disney built the empire he has today, he was fired by a newspaper editor because they said he lacked imagination and had no good ideas. In 1921, Walt Disney formed his first animation company in Kansas City. This where he made a deal with a distribution company in New York. He would then ship the New York company his cartoons and get paid six months later. He was forced to dissolve his company and didn't even have money for rent. He reportedly survived by eating dog food. Also, when Walt first tried to get MGM studios to pick up Mikey Mouse in 1927, he was told that the idea would never work. MGM was sure that a giant mouse on the screen would terrify women. As we know today, Walt Disney is famous for many cartoons, movies, and theme parks that continue to live on for new generations to enjoy. Walt Disney's confidence in himself never changed, and he didn't let doubts alter his path.

See, you are not alone in your struggle to create a stable life for yourself. People all through history and in all walks of life have been battling doubts and risking it all to make their dreams come true. Believing in yourself and fully committing to your seeing your dream through is one of the first steps to becoming an entrepreneur. You can't let the fear of failure stop you.

I know that's easier said than done. But there are some key characteristics that each entrepreneur or successful person has. Let's discuss seven of these traits now.

The first is being self-motivated. This is the most important trait in becoming an entrepreneur because you will be your own boss and have to tell yourself what to do. No one is going to do it for you.

A great example of this is Benjamin Franklin. He was highly self-motivated. He was forced to drop out of school at the age of ten to work full-time in his father's candle and soap shop. Did he let his lack of formal education fill his mind with doubts and quit trying to learn? No, he was so self-motivated that he taught himself to read and asked questions about many things. He strived to learn all that he could from the world as he worked in his father's shop. He spent all his free time reading and expanding his knowledge. When he got older, Benjamin Franklin apprenticed at his brother's print shop, where he learned a great deal about newspaper publishing. There, he also learned about politics and published his own work advocating for free speech.

His life was filled with achievements because of his self-motivation. He started what is now known as a library so that others could have resources to teach themselves and expand their consciousness. He also was a scientist who discovered the lightning rod and bifocals. Benjamin Franklin is also known as one of the Founding Fathers of the United States. How is that for not letting fear and doubt from a situation not hold you back? Benjamin Franklin is an amazing example of being self-motivated, and he didn't even make it past the 6th grade. He taught himself and worked hard to achieve his goals. Do you think he would have achieved half as much if he had spent his time waiting for someone to teach him or doubting his own ability? What an inspiration and confident person Benjamin Franklin! The self-motivation he showed at a very young age, should be an example as we strive to become self-motivated entrepreneurs.

The second trait of a successful entrepreneur is understanding what you can offer the world.

Fred Rogers knew that he could offer children a sense of love and confidence to feel special just as they are. He's famous for his iconic television show, *Mister Roger's Neighborhood*. But Fred Rogers grew up a child who struggled with obesity. He was often called 'Fat Freddy' and teased by his peers. You and I can both imagine the doubts and lack of confidence that this put in Fred Roger's mind. Once he entered his career on television, though, he turned his doubts and pain from his childhood into his life's work. He created *Mister Roger's Neighborhood* wanting to offer children a new type of television show. In his sincere way and fun songs, he reminded children that everyone is different, and everyone is special. He taught children to treat everyone as neighbors or with respect, as well as ways of coping with many feelings that everyone feels at times. Covering many touchy topics, Fred Rogers worked to make everything manageable just by being able to talk about it. Fred Rogers knew what he could offer the world and what he envisioned, and he was not willing to change his path based on what others were telling him. His show is still playing today and has inspired the new series, *Daniel Tiger's Neighborhood*.

Fred Rogers understood what he could offer the world, and he has helped others across many generations. We each are given different gifts, and we can find ways to help others and ourselves when we focus on using our gifts in our business.

The third trait is taking a risk. You will never succeed if you never try. Sometimes the best opportunities come from taking a chance or risking it all. That's what Steve Harvey did. Steve Harvey spent twelve years struggling to make it as a stand-up comedian. When he won a $50 prize for his comedy routine in 1985, Steve Harvey quit his job at the insurance office. He was married with twins that he was supposed to be supporting, but he felt he had to take this chance, or he'd always be wondering what if. He left home and lived out of his Ford Tempo, using a cooler as a refrigerator and eating mostly bologna sandwiches. He'd shower in rest stop bathrooms or hotel restrooms as he traveled the country to compete in every stand-up comedy contest he could. Most of his winnings from these contests, going to supporting his wife and family, Steve Harvey survived on only $50 a week. While fear might stop some people from taking the chance or make them run back to the security of a regular paycheck, Steve Harvey refused to give up. He spent years chasing his dream. In the early nineties, Steve Harvey finally got a break. He was cast on Showtimes *At the Apollo.* The success he had with this show led to him being offered other television opportunities until he got his own network show, *The Steve Harvey Show,* in 2012. His determination to pursue his dream led him to be a millionaire comedian, author, and actor. He took a risk and now has a great success story that he shares with the world.

Have the confidence that Steve Harvey had in himself and take a risk to start your own business.

The fourth train is knowing how to network. I know some days I just don't feel like talking to people. But being willing to talk to people and learn what they do can help you create connections as you start your business. You never know when you might need new expertise or when the person you meet could help you achieve your dream. Networking is also important for entrepreneurs to get their names out to others. The more people you tell about your business, the better chance there is for you to gain loyal customers.

Mark Zuckerberg knew how to network and used his contacts to pursue his dream. From an early age, he loved computers and was soon the go-to computer programmer on Harvard campus, even though he was just a sophomore. His two programs, which were called CourseMatch and Facemash, were very popular, but Harvard called them inappropriate and shut them down. Mark Zuckerberg dropped out of college after this. He pursued ways to create the site he had in mind full time. Based on his Harvard connections, he and his friends created a social networking site that allowed Harvard students to connect with each other. Mark Zuckerberg had a partner that was working on this with him, but when the initial model didn't work, the partner dropped out. Mark was back to the starting point, and he was doing it alone. His connections from Harvard allowed him to partner with Peter Theil, one of PayPal's founders, to continue building the social media platform. This was the site that changed social media forever in 2004 and what we now know as Facebook today. Mark Zuckerberg's Facebook reported earnings in September 2019 of $1.62 billion. Imagine what would have happened if Mark had stopped trying. Imagine what would have happened if he hadn't networked so well with the others at Harvard. Networking is an important step to being an entrepreneur.

The fifth trait is having basic money management skills. Being an entrepreneur means you are in charge of the business, so you have to be able to handle the finances. You have to know how to budget and be willing to investigate the most cost-effective way of running the business. I'm sure you have heard songs from the famous musician Ed Sheeran. Even though he has achieved great fame, he still gives himself an allowance. He doesn't believe in being wasteful. He has a Barclay student account and hasn't it because he doesn't want to be able to spend all his money at once. This Barclay student account allows him to give himself an allowance. He tries to spend only $1000 a month and says most of his money is used on taxis. Ed Sheeran is famous for staying in other people's houses as a way to save money. He spent a long time crashing in Courtney Cox's spare room.

Ed Sheeran is a great example of knowing how to manage money. Even though he has achieved great success, he isn't spending his money in excess. We can all learn a lesson about money management from Ed Sheeran and use it as we run our business.

The sixth trait is having flexibility. Just like in life, your business may not always go the way you planned. You have to be flexible to handle the new situation, especially willing to change when receiving negative feedback. Proctor and Gamble gained a lot of negative publicity in 2010 because they were defensive about bad reviews instead of flexible to investigate the cause of the bad reviews.

This negative attention crisis started after they launched their newest diaper. The negative reviews and comments gained momentum and soon spilled over from social media to the mainstream news. The company could have handled the situation better. First off, after the negative attention spread to the news, there were calls for Proctor and Gamble to apologize. However, this isn't what the company did initially. Instead, they gave media interviews while on the defensive and defended their product as safe and functional. This initiate response by Proctor and Gamble of insisting there was no evidence to support the allegations, and their product was safe, appeared to be a company that was protesting too much. The company did shift their response and become more flexible, but this was after the negative publicity had spread even further. In the next media interview, the company representative explained that many within the company were parents themselves, and they'd pull any product from the shelf if they believed it was unsafe. This shows how slow Proctor and Gamble was at getting the company's front lines the information that they needed to respond appropriately. The workers on the front lines didn't have the authority to do anything other than defend the product. Once the negative publicity reached the upper levels of the company, then the management changed their stance and showed flexibility. They created a turning point in this crisis by getting the angry customers, their opposition, on their side to help fix the problem. This did two things. One, it removed the negative energy that had been feeding the media stories. Two, it boosted Proctor and Gamble's reputation by showing the company's flexibility and willingness to listen to their adversaries. This flexibility allowed Proctor and Gamble to regain its positive image and continue to be a successful company. So being flexible is important in all businesses, especially when it comes to listening to product reviews.

The seventh and last trait that we are going to talk about is passion. Passion is important in life, but especially when you are starting your own business. I know everyone enjoys doing something that they are passionate about much more than something they have no interest in. When you are passionate about something, you will put more energy into it and have a higher motivation to succeed. Apathy lowers your motivation and fills you with doubt. Passion allows you to have a clear vision of what you want and set clear goals for yourself. The clarity will give you confidence and push doubts from your mind. You will be more motivated to succeed because you have the mind power to think and act intelligently instead of stressing over doubts and fears. Really wanting what you are working toward helps you stay motivated even when facing obstacles or setbacks. On the other hand, when you are not passionate about your goal, your mind is full of doubts and fears. This hinders your ability to focus. You spend all your time having your thoughts jump from one fear or doubt to the other. This leads to a very stressful life.

Strive to find your passion and, create a solid plan for each of them, and begin working towards achieving your dreams. Your passion will drive your motivation to new heights so you can achieve greatness.

Let's learn more about Jim Carrey, whose passion for comedy kept him motivated through his struggles and allowed him to reach success.

Born in Ontario, Canada, Jim Carrey was in a lower-white collar class family. His dad was a performer and a bookkeeper and was the provider of the family. In any case, he before long lost his employment when Jim was as yet a little youngster, and the departure of a steady salary drove the family to get destitute. For quite a while, the family needed to live in a van. This drove Jim to take quit school at 15 years old so he could take on a vocation as a janitor to help his family.

After two years, in 1979, Jim left his activity as a production line janitor and started doing comedy acts. He began to get by as the initial represent Buddy Hackett and Rodney Dangerfield. In 1983, Jim moved to Hollywood, where he featured in a TV film "Presenting... Janet." This was the start of an effective vocation for Jim.

It wasn't until his job in the 1994 parody Ace Ventura: Pet Detective where he had the option to score his greatest break, however. Jim was found and appreciated by numerous crowds for his profoundly expressive face, his master comedic abilities, and his trademark humorous character. Before long, more undertakings began coming in.

He won his first honor – the Golden Globe for Best Actor – for his job as the lead character in The Truman Show (1998). Not long after that, he packed away his second Golden Globe for his delineation of Kaufman in Man on the Moon (1999), in which he co-featured with Courtney Love. During that time of Hollywood victories, Jim Carrey immediately got one of the most generously compensated on-screen characters in the business.

His energy for parody acting despite everything blossoms with, and in spite of early difficulties, he didn't surrender. On occasion, when he may have had questions, he didn't let those keep him down. Envision the certainty help he got when he accomplished his fantasy. Presently, Jim Carrey is a symbol for all thing's parody, one of the top-earning on-screen characters in Hollywood, and is a double-cross champ of a Golden Globe. We can learn a lot about passion and motivation from Jim Carrey's life.

Chapter 2 Fears

Remember: You are not a failure just because you failed.

Acting despite fears is an ability that all entrepreneurs need to be able to do. One of my favorite quotes by Franklin D. Roosevelt talks about this same thing. He said,

"Courage is not the absence of fear, but rather the assessment that something else is more important than fear."

We all have fears—fear of failure, fear rejection, fear of not being good enough, fear embarrassment. It's part of everyone's human nature. We all want to succeed, don't we? I know I do. And yet, sometimes our fears are so overwhelming that we can't move forward. Our fears take over, and we don't admit that our goals are more important than our fears.

Eleanor Roosevelt is quoted as saying, "You gain strength, courage, and confidence by every experience in which you really stop to look fear in the face."

That means we have to make reaching our goals more important than our fears. Confident people don't stay in place because they are afraid. Entrepreneurs are willing to step out of their comfort zone and try their best to reach their goals, despite their fears.

It doesn't mean that you are going to succeed right away, but you can never succeed if you don't try. Don't let setbacks discourage you or make you fearful of trying again. I know it's easy when you have a setback, then you may start to see only the negatives in life. You might see this setback as something that you can't change. Doubts and fears grow quickly in your mind because of this setback, but remember, the setback is just temporary. Every setback can teach us lessons we can use to continue moving forward. Don't let the setbacks affect your health or change your plan. Use the mistake to your advantage and move forward in a smarter way. Learn from this setback so you won't be trapped by the same setback again in the future. In order for your business to succeed, you have to keep trying.

Let's look at the path Thomas Edison took and the setbacks and mistakes he learned from. Thomas Edison failed 1000 times before creating the lightbulb. If he had left his fears overtake him after he failed, Thomas Edison might not have become the prolific innovator we know him as today. Like most entrepreneurs, Edison was certain he could solve a fundamental problem he'd observed. In particular, Edison saw that at whatever point Congress decided on an issue, every representative would stand individually and get out his vote. To Edison, the wastefulness of such a framework was completely shocking, and he understood that he could design a framework to rapidly count all the votes and avoid the pointless and inefficient advance of getting out votes. Like any great business visionary after the customary item-based model, Edison hopped directly in, fabricated the framework, and afterward brought his programmed vote-count framework to Congress. Envision Edison jumping up the means to the congressional workplaces anxious to show how he had tackled such a huge issue and energized for the result toward the finish of his difficult work. Presently picture his by and large astonishment when the Senators tuned in and afterward gruffly dismissed his development—they didn't need it. Like most business visionaries, Edison was certain he had watched a genuine market need. He was more likely than not been frustrated at the failure of his "clients" to see how he had spared them a long stretch of time by changing a wasteful and senseless democratic procedure.

Yet, the reality of the situation was that Edison hadn't approved his presumption that the congresspersons really needed a programmed casting a ballot framework. Indeed, as it turned out, there was a lot of legislative issues and posing in the calling of votes, and the Senators weren't going to surrender that framework. Thomas Edison didn't let his fears take over and stop him from trying. He learned from his mistakes and kept working toward his goals.

The first lesson Edison's failures teach us is to validate your assumption about what customers will buy. Luckily, as opposed to letting the disappointment alter his motivation and path, Edison kept his positive energy and suppressed his fear. He found two significant rules that permitted him to get one of the most acclaimed sequential pioneers ever. To start with, he took in the pivotal need to comprehend your clients—explicitly the activity they are attempting to complete and why. After that experience, Edison reframed all his future endeavors with one straightforward expression, "I never need to assemble something that no one needs to purchase."

Second, Edison took in the estimation of quickly repeating to get to the arrangement clients required. For instance, in building up a financially suitable light, Edison really experienced more than ten thousand models before taking care of business. Had Edison followed the customary model of item advancement, his rivals would have beat him by decades. Later Edison got renowned for saying, "I have not bombed multiple times. I have not flopped once. I have prevailed with regard to demonstrating that those 10,000 different ways won't work. At the point when I have killed the ways that won't work, I will discover the way that will work." You will discover a way that works, as well, and I'm eager to give you increasingly explicit instruments, layouts, and practices to direct you to your large development.

Pioneers change the World and keep changing It

As a last note, let me raise my glass to every one of you who advance—as business visionaries, as administrators, as people, as families, or whomever you are. Pioneers change the world in little manners and huge ways. I love to see you do it, and in the event that I can support, fantastic. In the event that I simply get the chance to see you do it and be propelled, magnificent. Regardless of whether you locate a superior method to improve your life or an approach to improve the lives of many, continue attempting. You will completely change you and dig into improving things. I can hardly wait to see it. On the off chance that you don't think you are a business visionary or a trend-setter, I'll put my cash down that you are and can be.

Thomas Edison's excursion to getting perhaps the best stock in history wasn't simple, yet he never surrendered or quit attempting. His excursion has numerous extraordinary exercises about not letting questions, and your own suspicions control your brain. Edison kept his psyche concentrated on his objective and indicated his certainty just as his cerebrums for an incredible duration. Fears are a natural part of everyone's daily lives, but to succeed as entrepreneurs, our passion and motivation for success have to be greater than our fears.

One of the easiest ways I've found to do this is to focus on one task at a time instead of the outcome. Instead of worrying about the outcome, focus on the task at hand. This allows you to focus your energy on the task and keep your fears in check. I tend to take this to the extreme and develop deep tunnel vision, not wanting to do anything else. When you keep your mind on the task at hand only, you can focus your energy on creating a plan and following the steps necessary to excel. This will help you ensure that each step is done right because your energy is devoted to that step and not battling your own fears. Once you have your fears under control, there will be no stopping you on your path to becoming an entrepreneur.

Chapter 3 Knowledge

Knowledge raises your confidence and increases your ability to succeed. Ignorance fills you with doubt and hurts your ability to succeed.
The most important knowledge we can have as we start a new business is knowledge of ourselves. If you find yourself not able to be honest with yourself, or realistic about what your abilities are, then you need to gain this knowledge first. Enjoy getting to know what you do and don't know. It might help you to keep a journal of your thoughts. Ask yourself questions that you don't know the answer to. Then research until you find the answer. Teaching yourself something is another great way of increasing your knowledge and will boost your confidence in your abilities. Embrace the knowledge and start questioning and learning about everything in your life. It

will give you a new perspective on your environment as well as a sense of wonder and curiosity. The more you study and learn from the items and the people around you, your confidence will increase.

This knowledge of yourself will give you the ability to gauge what you need to learn as you start your business. Why does this work? Because of the old saying, knowledge is power. You are teaching yourself what you don't know. You are learning that your environment is filled with wonder instead of fear. It is the fear and unknown that makes people fearful and fills their minds with doubts. When fear and doubts take control of your mind, you don't have room for anything else, especially the brainpower and motivation it takes to run a successful business.

Sometimes knowledge and the opportunity to learn comes from unlikely situations. This is the case with Malcolm X. He was born Malcolm Little, is best known for his political views. His childhood was filled with experiences that gave him reasons to have doubts and fears. His father was killed, his mom was in and out of mental hospitals, and from a young age, he was in a series of foster homes. His confidence was shaken by this upbringing, and he ended up in prison when he was twenty. His time in prison, though he served as a useful turning point for him. While he was locked up, he got to know himself, figured out a goal and path for himself, and spent his time reading books from the Charlestown State Prison library. He studied a wide range of topics, including Islam. By the time he was released, his confidence was boosted, and his fears and doubts were under control. He would use the knowledge he had acquired in prison on Islam to form the foundation of his political beliefs.

Jack London, known for his books *Call of the Wild* and *White Fang,* also didn't have a traditional education and childhood. Jack London lived a childhood in poverty. He attended some school but was mostly self-taught by reading books at the Oakland library and asking especially the librarian questions. While Jack London seemed to display a lot of confidence at a young age, his fears and doubts caught up to him. He ran away to live a sailor's life at seventeen years old. Obviously, life at sea gave Jack London time to reflect on who he was, change his mindset and energy, resolve his fear and doubts by setting a clear path, and have the motivation to move forward. When he returned, he would complete high school and a year at a university. If it were not for all the library books he had read, Jack London's higher education might not have been possible. He gained knowledge from books and used them to succeed.

Edith Wharton was born into a wealthy family, but because she was a girl, she wasn't sent to school. It was common this time that a young lady was expected to spend her time learning manners and homemaking skills. Edith Wharton didn't show doubt and fear, though, instead at a very young age, she showed confidence and had a strong desire for knowledge. She began reading all the books in her dad's library and working on lessons on her own. Her reading expanded her knowledge and boosted her confidence even more because she would write hundreds of stories, books, and essays. She showed incredible motivation to succeed, and the knowledge she gained from books allowed her to. She would win the Pulitzer Prize for her novel *The Age of Innocence,* making her the first woman to receive that honor.

Ray Bradbury, an acclaimed sci-fi writer, got his passion for writing from reading books at his local library. He did attend formal schooling through high school but opted not to go to college. Ray Bradbury never doubted his decision not to attend college because he had a clear path and knew he was still capable of gaining the knowledge he needed. He spent the next ten years teaching himself about writing and the world. By the end of the ten years, he had read every book in the library and written thousands of short stories. What self-confidence he had and how much his motivation to succeed must have been to have acquired all that knowledge on his own. It was at UCLA's Powell Library that Ray Bradbury wrote his most famous novel, *Fahrenheit 451.*

Knowledge can be gained in many ways, but the most important knowledge you need to have is a true understanding of yourself. Knowing yourself this well will give you confidence in your abilities and a love for yourself that will motivate you to start your business.

Chapter 4 Faith

I am a firm believer that putting God first in your life is a major key to success. I have seen God pull me through some very challenging and horrible times in my life. He is the one constant in an otherwise unstable world. The unconditional love that God offers, though, can be used as a great motivator for you as you start your business. I think of this often, because no matter how much I am doubting myself, God still loves me and is there for me. The Bible teaches believers to follow the Ten commandments giving them a moral compass that detects the presence of evil. In life and in business, it is important to differentiate between good and evil. The Bible can be every entrepreneur's road map on how to run a business and live a positive life. It gives us a direction to follow with good standards and values.

A big part of faith is trusting in God's timing. Turning to him in every situation and then having the patience to wait for his answer and his timing. I'm not to say that this is easy for believers to do, I know I struggle with this a lot. Patience isn't always easy for me. We are human and struggle with the desire to fulfill our own selfish notions on our own timeline. It takes practice for Christians as they train their consciousness to be sensitive to God and grow their desire to follow the Bible's teachings. The Christian's consciousness becomes aligned with God's directions, and their desire grows to follow His path. Not to say that Christians can find all the answers in the Bible or see all the reasons for God leading them on their path. Believers do get angry at God because they are human. Depending on the strength of their faith, they may rebel against the conscious knowledge of God for a time.

The faith of each Christian is a work in progress. The conscience state is always being trained and expanded. God is so above any human, so advanced to any human understanding that a Christian is continually learning and growing across their life. We must make an effort in order to walk with God. However, at that same moment, we shouldn't judge others and should be conscious of their behaviors and thoughts. At every moment in our daily lives, the conscience is an invaluable aid to us in business and in our personal lives.

I know I find comfort from the path and guidelines that God gives me in the Bible. I have turned to the Bible and prayer many times when I felt doubt and fear about starting a business. The Christian movie producers, the Kendrick Brother's produce movies that inspire other viewers and me to trust God, will help you achieve your dreams. The movies depict how powerful faith in our lives can be. Their latest movie, Overcomer, gives another example of overcoming a physical barrier and finding faith in God. The heroine, Hannah Scott, is a fifteen-year-old student with asthma. She has many doubts about herself and about her purpose in life. She doubts her worth but is led to Christ by her school principal. Hannah's newfound faith gives her a new love for herself. She knows is she's a good runner despite her asthma, and she decides to join her school's cross-country track team. Even though her coach doubts her ability to run, she doesn't quit. Hannah shows great growth in faith and personal confidence throughout the movie. Her faith allows her to improve her running ability and courage to face the other fears in her life as she trains for each cross-country competition. She not only succeeds in proving to her coach that she is capable of. She proves it to the state by winning the state competition. What a great example of using faith to overcome your doubts and not let anything stop you from achieving your dreams.

You may ask: "How might I have God's ceaseless direction?" The appropriate response is that if God is calling you to comprehend His fact, you have to react to that calling and look for Him. As you read your Bible, you will discover invaluable guarantees. Isaiah gives the accompanying: "Look for the Lord while He might be discovered, call upon Him while He is close. Let the fiendish spurn his direction, and the wicked man his musings; let him come back to the Lord, and He will show benevolence toward him; and to our God, for He will bounteously exonerate" (Isaiah 55:6–7).

As you implore—as you change your entire lifestyle to God's method of genuine progress—He will forgive you through the Savior of the world, Jesus Christ. God has guaranteed that He will show benevolence toward you and forgive you, in the event that you apologize and look for Him.

God gives us numerous guarantees of His proceeding and cherishing direction. For instance: "Trust in the Lord with everything that is in you, and lean not on your own comprehension; in the entirety of your ways recognize Him, and He will coordinate your ways" (Proverbs 3:5–6). God guarantees that He will coordinate your ways and that He will control you through life to satisfy your human potential and extreme fate. At the point when you go to an intersection and are confronted with a choice, supplicate and request God's will to be done in your life.

As Jesus guaranteed us: "I will never leave you nor spurn you" (Hebrews 13:5).

At long last, what is the correct objective of an effective Christian? The correct objective is the Kingdom of God! As Jesus said in Matthew 6:33: "Look for first the realm of God and His exemplary nature, and every one of these things will be added to you."

Could you truly make progress and succeed based on faith? As the Apostle Paul expressed in Philippians 4:13: "I can do everything through Christ who reinforces me." The Bible uncovers the inconspicuous, changeless laws of life. At the point when we are in amicability with those standards and directions, we are honored. Indeed, from the earliest starting point of the Bible as far as possible, you will find that compliance with God's lifestyle brings gifts, and rebellion to God's lifestyle brings curses. The world's standards for progress: assets, force, position, and delight— - just bring torment, enduring, disappointment, and demise. The individuals who characterize accomplishment as "stretching out beyond" others, and participating in a narrow-minded guilty pleasure, won't just damage others; they will look at last mischief themselves. Genuine progress and success in our life come just through the Savior of the world, who instructed us to cherish our foes, set out our lives for each other, and live by each expression of God. At the point when we do this through the intensity of the Holy Spirit, we can live genuinely positive, motivated, profitable and successful lives, since we will help other people into the group of God, and into the Kingdom of God.

My faith is extremely important in helping me run my business and manage my life. I see God working in my life every day, and I know He can help you succeed as well.

Chapter 5 Mindset

Have you ever said things like, 'This just isn't good enough, I've got to redo this before anyone can see it,' or 'I won't start my business yet because I'm not quite ready,' and 'other people do that far better than me so I won't put my hand up?'. These are all forms of doubt that we tell ourselves to stop ourselves from acting. It's a method we use to try and protect ourselves from failure and embarrassment, but what are these doubts doing? Have you ever watched an interview with basketball star Michael Jordan? His tone throughout his interview displays his confidence and his positive mindset. Even when he talks about the failures he endured before his success, his tone doesn't change. He talks very openly about his 300 lost games and missed championship opportunities. His tone doesn't become angry, and his voice doesn't raise in volume. Instead, his tone stays firm and positive as he attributes his success to the lessoned from his failures. While some people are discouraged by failures, Michael Jordan shows us the right mindset to have regarding failures. To him, this is his recipe for success, and we should make it the recipe for our success too.

Keeping a positive mindset allows us to objectively look at a situation. Focusing on our emotions and fears only puts up barriers in front of us.

Barriers are defined as a natural formation or structure that prevents or hinders movement or action. We can't start our own business if we are afraid to take the first step.

We have to break down the barriers that our fears and doubts have put in front of us so that we can develop the correct mindset. These statements that we tell ourselves out of fear or doubt is our rationalize our reason for not acting. We tell ourselves these statements so much that we believe them, and it affects our mindset. Doubts and fears have taken control of us, and we lose motivation to try, which means we will never succeed at entrepreneurs. That's not what you want, is it? Of course not. We have to break down these barriers if we want to change our mindset and our lives. We have to be aware of these lies we are telling ourselves and be determined to keep a positive mindset.

How do we break these barriers down? Like other changes in ourselves, our inner barriers aren't going to all crumble and collapse overnight. We are going to have to work on them. Let's look at five ways to help ourselves take these barriers down.

Remove your fear of failure

Most people get stuck in life because their fear changes their mindset. They hide behind the barriers they created for themselves, convincing themselves that they are protecting themselves. You need to understand that failure is not the end of the world; it is a sign that you are trying. Failures are lessons that can teach you what your mistakes are and what you need to know. Throughout life, you go hard times before you grasp the lesson.

Failure is a basic part of life. You are not the only one to fail at something. Everyone does. You need to fail before you can succeed. There is no way to succeed at everything without failing at least once. Don't try to avoid failure by rationalizing your reasons for staying where you are. Instead, embrace failure as a guide that will help you on your path to success. Once you have changed your mindset on fear, you will be able to take the next step.

Do what you are afraid of

We are all afraid of something. It could be a fear as broad as a failure in general or something smaller and more specific, like heights, spiders, or change. Our levels of fear all differ, and how much they control our mindset differs too. Don't let your fears change your mindset and give you so much doubt that you can't take the next step.

Try exposure therapy, which suggests that you are exposed to what you fear in small doses in a controlled environment. This allows you to gradually get over your anxiety by making it something you do regularly and change your mindset.

As with anything, we have to practice facing what we are afraid of. This will help you get over your fear. For instance, talk to someone you trust about your business ideas.

Use your doubt as motivation

Having a bit of doubt can be useful in some cases. Doubts are an indication that you are stretching yourself with a new experience that takes you out of your comfort zone.

Being innovative and original means, you have to do something unexpected and new. When you go beyond what you are comfortable with, you learn about yourself as well as the world around you.

Doubts help you anticipate, plan, and see possibilities. They will encourage you to explore your options and dig for more knowledge. Great innovators use what has already been done as a starting point to create something new. They don't let their personal doubts stop them from achieving great things.

Check your reality

How we perceive our world isn't always accurate. We all make assumptions about what others think about us. We sometimes let these assumptions create fear in us. When enough fear enters our minds, it takes control of our mindset and actions. What is worse is that most of our assumptions are false.

You need to adjust your perception so you can see clearly what the world really thinks. Confirming information is one way to do this. Do you doubt your ability to succeed in your new business? Find another person who can tell you the truth and teach you how to improve. You can always benefit from a mentor or personal coach. We can learn a great deal from others and gain the assistance we need to improve ourselves.

Once we have changed our thinking on failure, the mental barriers we had up will begin to come down. We will be slowly taking control of our minds again by proving our doubts and fears wrong. We will be gaining confidence and learning lessons in our journey that will help us to live with a positive mindset.

A great way to easily boost your state of mind is to think of your past accomplishments. Be proud of your accomplishments. Use this positive energy to move forward and achieve the next step to owning your own business.

Not all barriers we face are in our minds. Some people have physical barriers that hinder their ability to achieve goals. But we can learn a great lesson on having a positive mindset from these people. They don't let their physical barriers stop them from achieving their dreams.

Richard Branson, the owner of Virgin Group or Virgin Atlantic Airlines, has had Dyslexia since childhood. Dyslexia is a learning disorder where a child has difficulty learning to read, talk, write, and spell words. It is a reading disorder that affects an aspect of the brain responsible for processing language. Richard Branson had Dyslexia, which resulted in poor grades in school. His headmaster at school, Robert Drayson, saw something unique or different about Robert that made him tell him he would either become a millionaire or end up in prison. Robert Branson chose to keep a positive mindset and is now a billionaire! His parents' support of his entrepreneurial drive played a big role in his positive mindset.

Richard Branson started his own business during childhood days at age 16 when he founded a magazine called the *Student*. He moved from here to found many other magazines afterward. Even the challenges can be the best in their chosen field.

Richard Branson is famous for creating the Virgin brand name, and many people don't know about his dyslexia struggles, so they can't appreciate how strong his abilities and his mindset really are. Disabilities don't have to hold you back and shouldn't change your mindset.

Another great example of overcoming barriers is Albert Einstein. He didn't speak until he was four years old, yet he didn't let that hold him back. He showed great confidence and a positive mindset throughout his life and is remembered for his theory of relativity.

It is inspirational to think that such a big name in the world of science struggled to learn and speak but is now one of the most well-recognized scientists in the world. His contributions to science make him one of the most renowned figures in history. So, let's learn more about the problems Einstein faced during his childhood.

Albert Einstein showed from an early age that he was a slow learner. He took over four years to learn how to speak, which bothered his parents and forced them to consult a doctor.

He was a below-average student in school spent a lot of time being scolded by teachers.

Einstein's father saw Einstein becoming an electrical engineer, but that wasn't Einstein's plan. He refused to take admission in electrical engineering and resented on the educational method of the institute. Einstein had a great imagination and saw visually instead of seeing words. He presented a theory of relativity, thanks to his imagination and determination. He kept a positive mindset, even after many failures.

It was in 1905, Einstien graduated but didn't get his doctoral dissertation accepted, yet he still produced four papers that changed the foundation of physics.

His papers were on light as particles or waves, and analysis of the existence of atoms, the theory of relativity, and his famous energy-mass equation.

He struggled throughout his early days and continued to step towards his goal no matter what the situations were. Albert Einstein went on to become the best scientist in the world up to now. He never let doubts stop him and showed great self-confidence. Albert Einstein thought about things and looked at things differently than other people and never accepted traditional wisdom. What a great lesson we can learn from his life. He had a great mindset to achieve what he wanted. We need to imitate his mindset as we move forward with our own businesses. Other times, physical barriers come to us in the form of an injury. This injury will hinder us from moving forward for a time. It's our mindset during the injury, and what we do after the injury is healed that determines if the barrier stays or goes away.

A recent example of this is the knee injury that Jaylon Smith of the Dallas Cowboys suffered in college. Smith's past is well-documented by now. He was the number one linebacker in the country as a junior at Notre Dame. People projected Jaylon to be a top-five NFL draft pick. Then, he suffered a devastating knee injury halfway through the first quarter of the 2016 Fiesta Bowl against Ohio State. He'd never previously missed a game or a practice until that injury occurred. He participated in every practice and game in high school at Bishop Luers in Fort Wayne, and in college for the Fighting Irish. Then with eight minutes left in the opening quarter, Jaylon

Smith landed awkwardly on his leg after getting shoved by Buckeyes' offensive lineman Taylor Decker.
He underwent reconstructive surgery on his anterior cruciate ligament and the knee's lateral structures. He wears a brace in practice to help him use his left foot because of the peroneal nerve damage the injury caused. He wasn't a top-five pick, but the Cowboys drafted Smith in the second round, even though they knew he'd miss the 2016 season. It took him until 2017 to get on the field in a game, but his patience and determination allowed him to succeed. He shows more confidence in his abilities and played every game in the 2018 and 2019 seasons. He is one of the best defenders on the team. Imagine if Jaylon Smith had given up on ever playing football again while he was recovering from surgery? He had to have plenty of doubts and fears, but he didn't let them alter his mindset or change his goal. As soon as he was able, he began striving to achieve his dream and play football in the NFL.
Surfer Bethany Hamilton's story teaches about barriers as well. In 2003, when Hawaiian surfer Bethany Hamilton was just 13 years old, she lost her arm in a shark attack while she was surfing in Kauai.
After losing nearly two-thirds of her blood, her life and future in surfing were in question. Surfing with one arm is a challenge, and doing so professionally nearly impossible. But Bethany Hamilton had a positive mindset and great determination to make it possible.
Her positive mindset has also given her a unique perspective on life after the attack, and she refused to let it change her path. Just 26 days after the attack, Bethany

Hamilton was back on her board, and two years after that, she was a national champion. What amazing determination and power of a positive mindset Bethany Hamilton showed. Her ability to keep a positive mindset should inspire us to take the next step toward owning our own business.

Stop waiting for the perfect

Waiting for the perfect timing is another barrier that keeps people from acting. Timing is such a small word, yet it has such a big influence on our lives. We base so many things on timing. We let our fears and doubts tell us things lie: "Now isn't the right time," "If only I had more time" or "Maybe next time." We let timing hold us back. This gives us an excuse not to move forward and not act. But our actions of waiting on timing is our fears and doubts controlling our mindset and our action.

I'm sure there are many of you that can think of a moment in your life where you were floating through life instead of living life. I know I have several periods of my life that I say that about. When bad things happen, or life doesn't go the way we plan, suddenly we stop trying. We are so let our fears and disappointments take over. And soon, we realize that we were waiting for life to happen, waiting for that so-called "perfect timing."

However, life is continuing, whether you like the current situation or not. Life isn't something that is going to happen for us someday or going to start once you have that new house, new car, next promotion, the perfect marriage, or when the kids get older. It's happening as I write this, and as you read this. This is life. Life is going one every day. Your real-life started the day you took your first breath. Therefore, every moment we spend waiting for the right time are moments, we could be using to build our own business and improve our own lives. We don't get any do-overs in life, so we have to live our best life every day and not wait.

Life shouldn't be spent fearing, hesitating, overthinking, and second-guessing. It's our self-doubt that allows us to convince ourselves that a day will come when we're 100% ready. But you will never feel completely ready. This is a perfect time, though, to take the next step to overcome your fear and doubt and start your own business.

No, the business isn't going to go according to our schedule, but we can gain confidence each time we reach one of our goals. It doesn't matter if it's earlier or later than we planned, we still achieved a dream.

Now that's not to say that sometimes, waiting is beneficial and necessary. A kindergartener can't say they don't want to wait 17 years to graduate college and skip directly to the college. This is not waiting for the perfect timing, but completing the necessary steps to achieve a goal. We can each be taking small steps toward our goals every day. We have to take control of our lives in the present moment.

What is holding you back anyway? Why not just go for it? Don't wait for a sign that the perfect time is here, don't let your doubts change your mindset and tell you aren't ready. Life is meant to be lived, so stop waiting and start your own business. Don't let moments pass you by. You never know if you might end up somewhere even better than you expected. The timing is now.

A great example of not waiting for the perfect time is the Gilmore Girls TV series shows. This show demonstrated a powerful message to women of all ages that one can accomplish anything if one tries and believes in one's self. Let's look at some lessons this show teaches us.

The first lesson the Gilmore Girls teaches us is that self-respect and a good mindset is everything. The show's relationship scenes between Rory and Jess characters throughout the series are a great example of this. Rory is attracted to Jess for his bad-boy image and initially enjoys his adventurous spirit. But when Jess ditched her to run off to Venice Beach without an explanation, Rory didn't wait for him. Yes, she was upset and disappointed, but she respected herself enough to know Jess didn't handle the situation right. She didn't let her pain change her mindset and deter her from her goals. Two years later, when Jess shows up at Yale and asks Rory to run away with him, Rory doesn't let her feeling for him takeover. She knows that he wasn't ready and would likely disappear on her again. She stands up for herself and repetitively tells Jess no. Though originally heartbroken, Rory didn't let the pain eat away at her, she didn't let her mind be filled with doubts, nor did she sacrifice her own goals to go back to the relationship. Rory kept her positive mindset and knew she could succeed without a relationship that wasn't right.

Chapter 6 Determination

Having determination is easy when everything is going smoothly, right? When we are enjoying success, we don't have to think about staying determined or continuing on our path. But when we start facing barriers or pressure, that's when determination becomes important. We can't let on failure stop us. Don't let one obstacle alter your determination. Success businesses face challenges, and business owners can be under a lot of pressure. We all know that pressure can be very hard to deal with. Most people see high-pressure situations as threatening, and fear makes them perform badly.

Seeing pressure as a threat changes your determination and alters your mindset. Pressure elicits fear of failure. It takes all your energy and impacts your short-term memory, attention, judgment, and spurs impulsive behavior.

The pressure causes our energy to be spent battling fear instead of building our determination and focusing on succeeding.

Next time you are facing pressure, try shifting your thoughts from seeing a high-pressure situation as a dangerous situation to seeing it as a *challenge*.

See how changing one word can alter our perspective on the same thing?

When you view pressure as a challenge, your mindset stays positive, and you're more determined to do your best. I don't know about you, but when I'm presented with a challenge, I throw myself into it, wanting to show everyone I can do it.

Practice changing the way you look at pressure. The pressure is an opportunity to grow and should increase your determination. The pressure is a part of business ownership, so we have to find a way to not let it affect our determination

You may be facing pressure that is a great opportunity for your business, but just remembers it's not the only opportunity you are going to get.

Keep a realistic perspective on this opportunity and others that you will have. This will allow you to stay focused and determined to succeed instead of being overcome with fear. Just remember all the famous people you have read about already that have failed many times before they succeeded. Missing one opportunity shouldn't alter your determination. You can and will succeed. You just have to keep trying and moving forward with your new business.

The idea of starting your own business can be intimidating. There is so much to do and think about, right? One of the easiest things I've found to help me is to focus on one small task at a time instead of the entire outcome. Once you have a business plan, break it into baby steps, and just focus on one step at a time. This allows you to be focused and determined on that task. I tend to take this to the extreme and develop deep tunnel vision, not wanting to do anything else until that task is completed. I stay more focused and determined than when I think of the big picture.

So what's the first step you can take toward starting your business? If it researching a space, developing a marketing plan, or developing merchandise, take it one step at a time. You will be surprised how fast you get to the overall outcome when you are determined to complete one step at a time.

By doing this, you are taking control of your focus and not letting fear change your determination. There are things we can control and things we can't control in every aspect of our lives. It's the same with starting a business. Control your mindset and your desire to keep moving forward. Don't let pressure or fear alter your path.

When you feel yourself losing your determination, think about your past success, this will *ignite confidence and renew your determination*. Don't think about your past failures. Only remember, *if* you did it before, then you can do it again. Once you're got your positive mindset and determination back, you'll be better able to take control of your fears and doubts.

It's no surprise that cultivating a positive attitude goes a long way toward achieving success. A positive attitude makes a big difference in your mindset and your determination and lessens the number of doubts you have.

Believing that you can succeed can prevent you from *focusing on doubts* that can drain and distract your working memory. Once doubts and fear are stripped from your mind, you are better able to act with determination.

Another part of keeping a determined mindset is not allowing yourself to get burnt out. When you're starting a business, you may be tempted to work on it 24/7. But doing this makes you prone to making careless errors. These errors occur because you are hurrying or because you are tired.

You need to take breaks, focusing on the here and now. You need to tune into your senses and just enjoy a moment of quiet.

You can relax by meditating or listening to music. I know both of these activities for me has a way of calming me down and letting me focus.

These little breaks can renew our drive and increase our determination when we go back to work.

It's natural to speed up your thinking, especially when you are excited about a new venture, but don't do it.

Don't hurry through the process of starting your business work steadily at it. This will keep your determination and mindset right throughout the process and allow you to avoid making errors. Unnecessary errors only cause us to have more doubts.

If your mind keeps doubting yourself, you won't be giving it your best effort and will lose your determination. You can only give the situation your full attention by keeping your brain rested and focused on the positive.

It takes a lot of confidence and determination to continue toward your goal even after being failing or being told no. We are going to look at some authors who had great self-confidence and a high level of determination to be able to continue after being told no. All of these authors did achieve their goal, and their perseverance paid off.

Stephen King was told no a lot before his novel *Carrie* was released. *Carrie* was the fourth novel Stephen King had written, and even he doubted at first that *Carrie* would be a success. *Carrie* started as a short story that he wrote for three pages before throwing it out. It was his wife, Tabitha, who encouraged him to expand the story of

Carrie into a full-length novel. Stephen King received a boost of confidence from his wife and now had a clear goal. He did write the full book, but his confidence was shaken again as he attempted to publish it. He was told no by thirty publishers. The note included in the rejection letter was 'we are not interested in science fiction which deals with negative utopias. They don't sell'. His fears and doubts must have wanted to take over, but Stephen King showed great confidence and stayed focus on his goal. Doubleday Publishing said yes and published a hardback version of *Carrie* in 1974. This book sold 13,000 copies as a hardback, and Stephen King started to doubt himself again. He thought the book had already run its course. But Stephen King was wrong, and the paperback rights were sold to Signet Books. What a confidence boost Stephen King must have gotten when *Carrie* went on to sell over a million paperback copies in the first year. Today Stephen King is a great example of keeping a positive mindset and being determined to achieve your goal because he has sold more than 350 million books. Mary Shelly's *Frankenstein* is now considered a classic, but her journey to publication was filled with obstacles. She completed writing her book when she was twenty years old and was told no by many publishers. She didn't let these rejects stop her, though, and her perseverance paid off in 1818 when *Frankenstein* was accepted by a small publishing company. The only problem was that Mary Shelley's name would not appear on the cover. The first run of the book only sold 500 copies. Many people's confidence would have been shaken, but Mary Shelley kept working toward her goal. In 1831 the book was heavily edited to make the story more conservative, which gave her commercial success. What an amazing lesson in confidence and determination we can learn from Mary Shelly, who's *Frankenstein* monster is one of the most iconic figures in horror history.

J. K. Rowling's debut novel, *Harry Potter,* has sold over 107 million copies to date, but success wasn't immediate for her. She was told no by twelve publishing houses. I'm sure her confidence was shaken. It is impressive that J. K. Rowling didn't let her fears and doubt overtake her. It was only when Alice Newton, the eight-year-old daughter of Bloomsbury founder, Nigel Newton, that led to Bloomsbury publishing *Harry Potter and the Philosopher's Stone*. Since the publishers were concerned that Rowling's books were geared to boys, they persuaded her to put J. K. Rowling on the over rather than Joanne Rowling. The publisher also advised J. K. Rowling to get a day job rather than rely on writing as a career. This had to create fears in Rowling's mind and doubt her ability. We all know what happened next, the Harry Potter series has sold 450 million books, had some of the highest-grossing films of all-time and has a huge following worldwide. J. K. Rowling's 'boy's book' has become universally enjoyed by people of all ages, genders, social classes, and cultures. Thankfully, J. K. Rowling had the confidence and the determination to continue trying. If not for her having this positive mindset, the world would never have enjoyed the *Harry Potter* series.

Chapter 7 motivation and drive

Step one to keeping your motivation and drive high is conquering your inner critic or that little voice in your head that says you aren't ready or aren't good enough. That voice is really your doubts and fears talking. If you begin listening to the voice, then soon you are going to be paralyzed by fear and completely off course from your goal. Don't let these voices change your motivation and drive. There are several steps you can take to overcome these voices so you can continue on our path to building your business. First, try to understand what your inner critic is telling you. Remember that your inner critic is your thought process. Use it to help you build a better plan not to stop your course of action. Two write down your negative thoughts in the second person instead of first-person. By replacing the 'I" with "you" in the statement, "I can't do anything right." It helps you see the ideas as an outside point of view, "You can't do anything right." This makes it not a direct statement from you. If you imagine it's someone else telling you these things, it becomes like a challenge or dare. For me, that would be a huge motivator to prove them wrong. With this motivation, you can respond to your inner critic by writing realistic and positive statements about yourself, such as "I may have set back, but I'm smart and able to achieve this goal." The most important thing is to remember not to change your goal or stop trying because of your inner critic. Take actions to put these doubts into positive actions and continue toward what you want to achieve.

Rocky Balboa's famous quote is, "You don't always have to win to win." The story of Rocky Balboa tells a motivational story of an underdog struggling to fight his way through life in the boxing ring. He never lost his motivation to continue the thought, whether it is in the ring or life, challenged him to develop his character and increased his motivation. Rocky didn't let his self-doubt take control of his mind. He didn't get angry at himself and stop trying.

We all know it's difficult to start new habits when old ones are so deeply ingrained. Thankfully, JAY-Z doesn't listen or limit himself to this idea. He has shown great motivation and drives in his career. Since, at 47 years old, we saw the amazing rapper accomplish something he's never done: lock-in with one producer and make one splendid album. As we as a whole know, the rapper's amazing collection 4:44 was delivered by No I.D., the man who helped groom legends like Common and Kanye West. On this venture, you can tell they're pushing one another: Jay gives his generally genuine and fair presentation in years, while No I.D. gives Jay a portion of his most finished work.

In a profession that has traversed over 20 years, the craftsman has worked together with many makers. Be that as it may, there's just been a chosen few who have had an extraordinary bond with the incredible rapper. What motivation and drive Jay Z displays and a great example he is for us. He is showing us that he is acting in spite of fears by taking the step to find another producer for each album. He is also showing how important being motivated to work toward your goals is. He never gave up, and neither should you.

Now, let's look at Ellen DeGeneres. Ellen DeGeneres dropped out of the New Orleans university to work and find her true calling. She worked numerous odd jobs as she searched for the career she loved. She started performing comedy routines in local coffee houses at the age of twenty-three. She knew she'd found what she wanted to do, and she was motivated to succeed at it. She continued doing comedy routines and entering contests as her popularity grew. A turning point in her career was when she was invited to appear on *The Tonight Show with Jimmy Carson*. This opened the door for Ellen when it came to the television world. She was soon cast in other sitcoms and movies. Then in 1997, on the Oprah Winfrey show, Ellen DeGeneres opened up about her sexuality. After coming out as a lesbian, Ellen DeGeneres became someone everyone was talking about, and not in a flattering way. She struggled to find any work as the press and people continued to make cruel jokes about her. Ellen DeGeneres continued to pursue another television or movie appearance and found she was altering her dress and hairstyle to appear the way society wanted her to appear, more feminine. Ellen DeGeneres was out of money and didn't know if she'd ever work again, but she continued working toward her goal. She slowly gained the confidence to be authentic, and she began to see people's reactions to her authenticity. It still took her years of rejection before she landed her daytime television show, *The Ellen DeGeneres Show,* in 2003. Her motivation and drive to continue despite failure and adversity paid off for her. Her show has won 38 Emmy Awards, including four for its host. She has had huge success. Ellen DeGeneres is now an activist for the LGBT community and married to the love of her life, Portia de Rossi.

Beating yourself up isn't going to give you the motivation to move forward. Instead, it is going to make you scared of failure and keep you stuck in place.

Instead of beating yourself up over your failure, make a list of your past accomplishments.   Hang this list in your home, where you will see it often. My list on the bathroom mirror, and I spend a few minutes every day reading the list. By remembering your past successes, you can keep your motivation to want to succeed again. You are using you're good feeling you got from past success to drive you forward and create new success.

Sometimes, though, you need someone else's energy and excitement to renew you. Let a trusted and admired person's motivation, enthusiasm, and constructive optimism flow over to you. Spend twenty minutes each day, getting encouraged by someone. It will keep you motivated to continue. Encouragement could come from talking to your best friend that you admire. Reading your favorite author's book on a topic you are struggling with. Listening to inspirational music. Or watching a course online. You'll feel better afterward and have a more optimistic outlook and a new motivation to continue.

Entrepreneurs have to be motivated to succeed. They are their own bosses and don't have anyone telling them what to do. Use these suggestions to find a way to keep your motivation and drive high as you build your business.

Chapter 8 discipline

Discipline is important. I remember I hated being told what to do when I was a child. I couldn't wait to grow up and be on my own. But, once I did get out on my own, I realized that I needed to have the discipline to tell myself what I needed to do. That is a lot harder sometimes. It takes a much stronger mindset to be able to have that level of self-discipline.

We all know we learn that children learn a lot of self-discipline and being mindful when they start school. Children have to pay attention to what the teacher is saying, not what the other kids are doing or what they see out the window. It is very hard for children to stay mindful while sitting still. This is why lower elementary classes consist of many different sensory activities. This helps the child to concentrate on each moment and learn from hearing stories, doing crafts, playing on the playground, and learning new skills.

As children continue to grow, they begin to learn to be mindful through the self-discipline of completing homework each night. They also learn to be mindful in new areas of life, such as playing an instrument or participating in a team sport. Both of these activities require mindfulness during them as well as the mindfulness to practice.

By participating in sports and learning to play music, we learn even more lessons in mindfulness and discipline. Because both of these skills require practice, they teach us to accept our mistakes. Instead, we grow in consciousness and mindfulness as we learn lessons from each of our mistakes. Music and Sports help us see that mistakes can teach us and help us improve, so we don't make the same mistake over and over.

Music and sports teach us discipline because there are specific steps we have to take to improve in each. In music, you start by learning notes and scales before moving on to learning songs. In sports, you start with learning basic skills and building endurance before you start in a game. These activities teach us self-discipline and the importance of practice.

Creed II actor Russell Hornsby was interviewed on the subject of confidence and discipline throughout his career. In his interview, he talks about taking ownership of every role he plays. Like anything else, acting takes practice. Practicing a skill every day takes a lot of self-discipline. There are days when he hasn't felt like practicing, but his self-discipline and motivation made him practice. He has seen the benefits he gained from practicing because the better he is, the more poise he can display when he walks on the set.

This poise or confidence that comes from owning the role. He can own the role because he was disciplined enough to practice his craft. This brings Russell Hornsby a sense of comfort and eases with each role. Russell Hornsby was glad he was able to own the role of Creed II. He explained how he got there by saying, "Twenty years of work is what prepared me for this role at this time."

Being disciplined enough to practice for what you want to achieve will not only help you get better at your craft, but as Russell Hornsby explained, it will also allow you to gain confidence. Creed II wouldn't be the same if Russell

Hornsby hadn't prepared for the movie so well. The scenes would not be believable, and the audience would be able to see his hesitation. Russell Hornsby showed great confidence in every scene of this movie. It is also comforting to know that this wasn't something that happened to him overnight. He's been practicing and working on his acting for twenty years. His story should inspire us to practice and be more self-disciplined.

Oprah Winfrey is 62 years of age. She is among the best business visionaries ever, with total assets of $3 billion. Life magazine has named Oprah the most powerful lady of her age. Business Week has named her the best African-American donor in American history. Oprah was raised by an unmarried adolescent mother, and they didn't have much money when she was growing up. She was explicitly manhandled all through her youth and turned into a disturbed, insubordinate young adult. She fled from home at age 13. Regardless of her troublesome childhood, Oprah didn't permit her past to decide her future. She was self-disciplined and motivated to work for what she wanted. She didn't let barriers or doubt stop her and shows us that we can accomplish anything through disciplined work and motivation to keep trying.

The mindfulness and discipline we have learned through other tasks in our lives can help us now. A big part of being disciplined is being able to set your life on the path you want and set goals for your self. Disciplined people realize that life is a work in progress and that opportunities for success and self-fulfillment are all around us. We just have to be willing to take that first step. To take that first step, we need to have a direction or goal.

As Alexander Hamilton said, "Those who stand for nothing fall for anything."

We need goals and a direction in life to move forward, and we need the discipline to keep working toward them. Disciplined people are not afraid to set goals, make plans, and then take steps to reach their goals. They don't doubt their path once they've started or let their fears of failure keep them from taking a step toward their goals.

Disciplined people also understand there will be some challenges and setbacks, and adjustments will have to be made. They use every challenge, setback, or barrier as a learning experience to help them turn their worst days into a success.

Let's use the self-discipline we have learned through life to help us start our own business. Entrepreneurs need to be able to pay attention to each detail so we will make fewer mistakes and learn more from each experience because we are in the moment. Fewer mistakes mean fewer doubts, and you will have more motivation to continue. What an important step to being mindful and disciplined in our daily life on our quest to starting our own business.

Chapter 9 Who you surround yourself with

Your mindset, motivation, and energy level are affected by many things. One of them being who you surround yourself with. We are greatly influenced by other people's attitudes, and that can affect our energy in a positive or negative way. When someone criticizes you or is always complaining, then it's easy to start doubting yourself and develop their negative attitude. On the other hand, if someone praises you and is optimistic in every situation, it is easy for you to stay motivated and feel positive.

Being around positive people helps to raise your motivation and increases your energy. Negative people drag you down and fill your head full of doubts. Remember your parents telling you to choose good friends? I'm sure you were also told you are whom you associate with. I didn't fully understand this until I was an adult, but I now see that the people we associate with are the ones who form us. Whether consciously or not, we learn from and try to copy the people we are around as we grow to find our own voice.

By seeking out positive, motivated people to associate with, this will ensure you are learning good habits and copying good behavior. They will be much more open and want to help you. You'll be able to talk to them, ask them a question, and enjoy their presence without having to be fearful of cruel remarks. Instead of filling your head with fears and doubts, their ideas will raise your energy level and encourage you to continue reaching for your goal. They will help you grow to be a more motivated and positive person and might even be able to help you in your business.

When you spend time with negative people, and you'll gradually sink to their level. Their thoughts will infect you, and instead of building you up will bring you down. You will grow to be dishonest, fearful, cruel, and lack the motivation to do anything.

Strive to learn and emulate people who are more motivated and positive than you. This will boost your energy and keep you determined to continue moving forward with starting your business.

Another aspect of how other people affect us is when we are jealous of angry. These thoughts often cloud our minds to where we are only focused on these negative feelings for another person. This isn't beneficial for us and results in us making poor decisions. It is also very draining and will cause you to stay in place instead of moving forward.

A classic example of how anger towards a person can affect your judgment is displayed in John Hughes's classic movie "Ferris Bueller's Day Off." This is one of my favorite movies, and I learn something new from it every time I watch Matthew Broderick. The 1986 classic story of a teenage boy, Ferris Bueller, who, decides to fake sick and enjoy the sunny weather. From the first scene of the film, Ferris' older sister Jeanie is angered by her folks' choice to permit her sibling to remain at home from school. All through the film, she becomes angrier as the school appears to be persuaded that her sibling has some perilous ailment.

In the wake of smoldering in an unfilled passage, she concludes that something must be done, and reality must be uncovered. Her arrangement, unfortunately, reverse discharges, and she winds up at the police headquarters to record a report against Mr. Rooney. He is likewise attempting to uncover her sibling. In the station, she meets Charlie Sheen, who winds up being insightful in spite of his "terrible kid" picture and offers some decision words: "You should invest somewhat more energy managing yourself, somewhat less time stressing over what your sibling does." Jeanie gives us a great example of how letting our anger and fear dictate our actions, clouds our judgment. Jeanie's mind was so focused on her anger that she didn't make a true plan to reveal what was going on with Ferris. Her mind was also not fully in the moment as she acted, which is another reason her plan doesn't work. The doubts and anger that filled her mind as she sat in the police station might have inhibited her from fully grasping the lesson Charlie Sheen's character was giving her.   It is a good lesson, though, and fits with the theme of this book. We need to be focused on improving ourselves and doing our best. We can't be confident of ourselves when we are worried about judging and correcting others.

You also shouldn't focus on comparing yourself to other people. This leads to self-doubt and a lack of motivation. Their successes, and especially to the high-light reels that they share on social media, make their life look easy. This makes you doubt yourself and question why you are struggling. Remember that these successes are only part of their story. You don't know what they had to overcome to get there. Instead, use their success as a motivation tool for you. Emulate their path or plan if their business is similar to yours.   Then find motivation by competing with yourself. Start challenging yourself to grow your business a little more each day or take another step each day. If you start comparing yourself and your business to where you were yesterday or in the past, you will see how far you have come. You will get an energy boost from seeing all the barriers you have overcome and the progress you have made. That's the comparison that is worth our time and attention.

Keeping a journal can be a good habit and help you have a record of the ways people affect you as well as track your success.

1. Keep a realistic record of your life. You'll have written memories of the positive people and things, the successes you have had. You'll also have written down how you overcome barriers and the positive energy that comes from that instead of just remembering the struggle.
2. It will help to give you clarity. It is often easier to be truthful and to gain clarity if you write out the issue on paper or in a computer document. It will allow you to work through a problem or understand how someone else is affecting you and is their effect good or bad. This is as beneficial as talking to someone else about your concerns. It's much better than if you try to go through it all in your mind. Writing it down, you will find you get both

sides of the situation as opposed to just the one that your mind is trying to sway you to believe.

You can look back through your journal when you doubt how far you've come and read the progress you have made. You can see how many people have helped you to succeed and see the ways which you associate with effect your mindset. I love writing down my successes and find it a way to celebrate life. I also write down my worst days and then revise them when I see a positive outcome from them. I write about people that motivate me to remind myself to emulate their good traits. Re-reading your experiences with different people will help you see how these people influence you.

I know there have been people in my life that I really liked being around, but after reading my journal entries about them, I realized that they were not the type of people I wanted to emulate. Continuing to associate with them was going to hold me back and have a negative impact on my success. If I hadn't written down my experiences with them, my mind would have continued to have me focus on what fun they were to be around. Journalling has allowed me to keep myself positive and motivated because I'm surrounding myself with people who inspire me. Try writing or journaling for yourself. I know it will help you too.

In life and especially as you start your own business, it is important to use other people's influence to build you up, not drag you down. We all have a great influence on each other's attitudes and emotions. Be and find people that make you feel good about yourself and encourage you to build your business.

Chapter 10 protect your energy

Energy raises your consciousness and gives you confidence. Disease fills your mind with fear and doubt. In order to have energy, you need to be healthy. Take care of your body, for it is your vessel to interact with the world. Energy gives you an ongoing flow of necessary life experiences. Energy is determined by what we eat. Do we fill our bodies with healthy proteins and vegetables? Or do we feed our bodies starchy fats and junk food? Start paying attention to how your food of choice will impact your body. Yes, that cookie and soda will give you a temporary burst of energy. Still, all that sugar can lead to diseases if consumed regularly. We might not feel the same burst of energy from eating that chicken breast and salad, but the energy from this food will be healthy and consistent without the negative peak and valley.
You need energy and a healthy body to experience life. Every life experience is a lesson or a way to increase your

consciousness. The more you experience and learn, the more confident you will feel. Maybe you aren't naturally a high energy person that wants to try new things. Maybe you are someone who is afraid of new experiences. You'll have to build up your energy level and tolerance for new experiences. Start with a new experience that will only take a short amount of time. This will allow you to increase your confidence and not overwhelm yourself. This will help you raise your consciousness. After a few experiences are under your belt, you will find you have more energy and look forward to these new experiences. You'll be growing in energy and motivation. But without energy, you starve your motivation and live in doubt.

The creator of "America's Got Talent," Simon Cowell has a motto, which is "Never Be Complacent." That motto has driven the 58-year-old mogul to success on both sides of the Atlantic, as founder and CEO of Syco Entertainment, a television and film production company that boasts a roster full of A-list artists and worldwide shows including "The X Factor" and "Got Talent."

Simon is the opposite of complacent and has high energy because of his positive attitude. He also is extremely motivated and not afraid to step out of his comfort zone. He's willing to fight for his dreams and to make his creative ideas a reality. He does not let doubt deter him from his path. His high energy allows him to think of new ways to make his show better, create new ideas for the show, and plan ahead in his life. What a great example Simon Cowell is for us. He truly is benefiting from the positive energy and motivation he possesses.

We all too often decide to blame others or our situation for our poor energy and motivation. This isn't healthy and will not give us the success we are wanting. What is important to remember is that we are in control of our lives and our path. We can take a bad situation or experience and use it as motivation to improve our life. When we succeed at doing that, we will feel more confident and improve our energy in a positive way.
A great example of being in control of your energy is Barak Obama. When Barack Obama's party lost control of Congress back in 2015, due to his lack of popularity nationwide, we couldn't see anything but confidence and positive energy in Barack Obama as he addressed the joint session of Congress. In every aspect of his presidency, Barack Obama showed confidence and often defiance as he led the nation. It was in Obama's tone and demeanor that we can easily see he had positive energy. He never doubted that his path to boost and strengthen the economy wasn't the best thing for the United States. The nation would never have followed him if we sensed he was hesitant or filled with doubt. Barack Obama is a great example of the energy and confidence it takes to be a leader.
There have been other people who are born or grew up in less than ideal situations, but have found motivation and positive energy in their lives and were able to succeed. Harriet Tubman was the fifth of nine children destined to a slave. Tubman and two of her siblings got away from subjection when she was 27. Her siblings returned and constrained her to come back with them. Not long after that, she got away again to Philadelphia, Pennsylvania,

without her siblings, utilizing the Underground Railroad, a casual, efficient arrangement of free blacks, slaves, and white abolitionists.

All through the Civil War, Tubman worked for the Union Army, first as a cook and nurture, and later as an equipped scout and spy. She was the principal lady to lead an equipped undertaking in the war, freeing more than 750 slaves in South Carolina into three steamers.

In her later years, Tubman ventured out to New York, Boston, and Washington, D.C., to elevate ladies' entitlement to cast a ballot. She went to gatherings of suffragist associations and worked close by Susan B. Anthony. At the establishing meeting of the National Federation of Afro-American Women, Tubman was the keynote speaker. Harriet Truman showed extraordinary positive energy and motivation to act in spite of her fears. And used her positive energy to stand for what she believed in regardless of what others thought.

Frederick Douglass was born in Maryland and was a slave. He didn't have an ideal childhood. He was separated from his mom at seven years old and afterward lived with his grandma.

He figured out how to read when he was around twelve. He accepted that the information he picked up from reading and used it to change his mindset. He knew that the knowledge from these books would assist him with moving from subjection to opportunity. This gave him a positive energy and motivation to succeed. Douglass attempted to get away from twice before he succeeded. He started going to abolitionist gatherings, and at one, he was out of the blue welcomed to talk. He was apprehensive, yet he was motivated and taught himself to talk. He remained positive that he would succeed. He was expressive to such an extent that he was urged to turn into an abolitionist subjugation speaker.

The first of three life accounts were distributed in 1845. In the wake of coming back to the United States, he distributed his first abolitionist paper. Douglass addressed against servitude and for school integration during the Civil War. From that point forward, he supported ladies' entitlement to cast a ballot. Frederick Douglass profited by his fearlessness and defeated numerous boundaries throughout his life. He wouldn't be recognized as a backer for ladies' privileges if he had let himself be filled with doubts instead of the motivation and positive energy he displayed.

Another way to keep your energy high and positive is to reward yourself often. We are all more motivated and have more energy when we feel like we are making progress. So, break down your goals of starting and running your business into baby steps that are easily attainable. When you've taken one small step forward, celebrate that small step. It is a win. Whether you set up your own website or secured your own studio space, you're done with the first step. Take confidence and energy from this win and be proud of yourself for taking the first step. You can celebrate this win by treating yourself to a tasty snack or your favorite dinner, spending time on your favorite hobby, or buying yourself something you've wanted for some time now. This will renew your energy, recharge your motivation, and boost your confidence. Your celebration will motivate you to continue because each small success is exciting and fun. And that will push self-doubts aside so that you can keep moving and get more small and bigger wins. You will be able to see results quickly, and that will only give you more energy. All this positive energy will enable you to start and grow your business so that your success story is the one people are reading someday.

Conclusion

As an entrepreneur, you have to consider how to continue in your business and be set up for numerous difficulties. Starting your own business gives you a feeling of opportunity and strengthening. You can fabricate things and watch them develop.

• Take a risk: The best business visionaries didn't get to where they are by avoiding any and all risks. As a business person, you have to face determined challenges for your business going ahead.

Facing challenges doesn't mean you are visually impaired in view of its piece of the activity! Effective business visionaries likewise realize which dangers taking and which they shouldn't. Figure out how to distinguish the dangers that will profit your business and take them. There are a few drawbacks to facing challenges. However, the benefits of having your open doors frequently far exceed the risks you take getting there. For example, you may choose to make an application despite the fact that there are numerous applications accessible. In the event that you think your application is better than others or offers something that others don't, do it.

• Plan your business: Before you start your business, you should have a strategy. The field-tested strategy defines its objectives just as its system for accomplishing those objectives. This arrangement is significant for drawing in financial specialists just as estimating the accomplishment of your business.

• Market your business: You have to concentrate on advertising previously, during, and after you start up your business. You may have the best Quests house in the city, yet in the event that you ought to have the option to concentrate your showcasing endeavors on your intended interest group. For instance, JUMIA might be bound to see a promotion via web-based networking media than on a midtown bulletin.

- Reduce doubt as a business person: Entrepreneurs should have the option to point and act immediately whenever they see a chance or perceive an error. As a business person, in the event that you let fear lead you, you won't have the option to tune in to your instinct, you will be reluctant to take the fundamental dangers, and your judgment will be ruined with feeling. Recall that dread is identified with your perspective. So figure out how to decrease and deal with your dread, and you will be a significantly more fruitful business person. As a business person, take a couple of seconds around evening time when you are distant from everyone else to consider the choices you have made that day that have come about.

Pondering the choices that you made that profited you, others, or your business will push you to rapidly assemble your certainty and lessen dread.

- Hire excellent workers: fruitful business people aren't effective inside an area. We, as a whole, have an extraordinary group and encouraging a group of people behind us. You need to recruit accomplices who have extraordinary aptitudes and whom you like and regard. You are bound to prevail with a co-worker, then you are on your own You and your workers will cooperate for quite a while and settle on upsetting choices. In the event that your accomplice has a character that you don't regard, your group won't keep going long.

- Plan your financing: arranging your financing is to fund your business so it won't crash! Numerous business visionaries invest a lot of energy searching for cash and insufficient acting. For most business people, they are utilizing their reserve funds to begin their business. Plan out your funds in the first place and attempt to adhere to it, however, realize that the arrangement should be adjusted en route.

- Listen to complaints: This is one of the tips that I believe is the most significant for business people to learn. Without clients, you can't have an effective business, and without the client's complaints, you can't perceive your shortcoming.

We made it through a lot of material and read a lot of inspirational stories of other people's success. I hope it has motivated you to start your own business and join the successful entrepreneurs of the world. Stay motivated and disciplined in achieving your goal of starting your own business. I know I'll be reading about your success story one day soon!

www.ingramcontent.com/pod-product-compliance
Lightning Source LLC
Chambersburg PA
CBHW071121240526
45465CB00022B/758